Marjorie White
Her Life and Work

Gary Olszewski

Published in the USA by:
BearManor Media
P O Box 71426
Albany, Georgia 31708
www.bearmanormedia.com

ISBN 978-1-59393-625-9

Printed in the United States of America.

Table of Contents

Dedicated to:
Every Working-Class Actor and Actress of the Stage and Screen,
Once Famous but Long-Forgotten

Thank You All.

I want to thank everyone, in no particular order, Three Stooges fans or not, for the help you've all given me the past few years in putting this work together: Gary Lassin, Frank Reighter, Gary Hammann, Rich Irwin, Cole Johnson, Rich Finegan, Bill Cappello, Rocky Miles, Jane Corey of the Catholic Centre Archives, Winnipeg, Carl White and Helen of the Greenwich Connecticut Library, Anne Young of the Greenwich Historical Society, Helen of the Homestead Inn, Greenwich, Carol Celentano of Fox Legal, the staff of the Margaret Herrick Library, UCLA, all the helpful people whose names I can't recall in the Manitoba Public Library, Sharon Foley, Idelle Talbot, Chris Kotecki and all others of the Manitoba Provincial Archives, Amy Bowring of Dance Canada Danse, Toronto, Stephanie Jones, (owner/curator of an excellent website on Joan Crawford), the staff of *Newspaper-Archive.com*, whose electronic databases on which I've drawn heavily, those also of *FamilySearch.org* for the same resources, the kindly people at the LDS Family Research Center here in Las Vegas for allowing me the use of their facility, Harry Preston, co-author of Thelma White's book, Sarah Jensen of Ontario Archives, and so many others whose names I've forgotten because I've had only 1-time or sporadic contact with, you all know who you are.

And last, but certainly not least, Ben Ohmart, Sandy Grabman, and Brian Pearce of BearManor Media, for their diligent work editing and putting this whole thing together for the world to see! Without their help, I'd continue on as the stereotypical "Starving Artist!"

But my most heartfelt thanks of all I must extend to Ms. Marcine Jones, of North Dakota, a distant cousin of Thelma White (Wolpa), for the personal family information she provided me with, irreplaceable one-of-a-kind historical treasures.

And to everyone else who has come to share my interest in Marjorie White's life and times.

Gary Olszewski

Introduction

We all know spunky, vivacious Marjorie White from her talented appearances in films like *Sunny Side Up, Happy Days, Diplomaniacs,* and *Woman Haters,* as well as a handful of other really awful films (a few of which are sadly lost forever. However, the question remains: "Who was she, and whatever became of her?"

What began as an idle curiosity about an obscure actress has led me, over the past few years, deeply into history: I've tracked her family's history back as far as the late 1600s, as well as detailed personal data on her life, and the lives of her three brothers and younger sister. The farther back I went, however, I realized that few, if any, readers other than myself would be interested in her distant ancestors, so the search through history suits my personal interest, with increasing zeal.

I've compiled a comprehensive biography of her to uncover who and what she was off the screen, in real life, as a woman, as well as a talented public performer. It's rather sad that her star billing in *Woman Haters* was the first and only time in her career she was credited over and above the other actors, her last film before her untimely demise in 1935. After the grueling years in Vaudeville, and six years in film, she was just on the verge of making it to the "big time" when death took her. (It's rumored that she was negotiating with, or had just signed a contract with, RKO Studios at the time, quite possibly the reason for the celebration that fateful night).

This work results from the examination of newspaper articles, reviews of her work, and her partner Thelma White's book, *Thelma Who? Almost 100 Years in Show Biz.* So as not to infringe on any copyrights, and more importantly, not to insult her or Thelma's memory, anything I quote verbatim/directly I disclose, in full, the source, author and date (if known). Also, government records, which I have unearthed, don't lie: this should serve to dispel any misconceptions concerning dates, places, and events of her life.

Come with me now, to take a look into the life of the *real* Marjorie White, from the very beginning. We'll examine, together, her family background, her childhood years at home, her stint with the Winnipeg Kiddies, one-half of the White Sisters duo and their subsequent career on the Vaudeville stage, and her less-than-glamorous few short years in the motion picture industry, as well as the day-to-day events of her personal life. I hope you will find her story as interesting and intriguing as I have. So let's step back to Canada more than 100 years in time, and begin there. Ready? Here is her true story.

Pacific Avenue, Winnipeg, about 1910.

William Avenue, Winnipeg, about 1912.

Her Family
and Early Childhood

Marjorie Ann Guthrie was born on Friday, July 22, 1904 — *not 1907 or 1908* — at 151 Main Street, Winnipeg, in the facilities of Dr. Charles Jamieson, in the Hespeler block, just west of the bridge at the north bend of the Red River. Her parents Robert and Nettie, both natives of Ontario and members of the Presbyterian faith[1] who married at Winnipeg in July of 1902, lived at 350 Pacific Avenue, a short distance away.

She was the first born of five children to the Guthries: brothers Orville, Morley and Stewart arrived in August 1906, October 1909, and 1913 respectively, and sister Belva in February 1915. As late as 1911 the family lived at Pacific Avenue; after that, documents show their address as 717 William Avenue.

But what of little Marjorie? What was she like as a youngster? It would seem, from all the extant research sources, both up-front and between-the-lines, that she was as much self-centered as self-confident, and truly enjoyed making herself the center of attention. It's as if she knew from the start what she had, and enjoyed showing off her inborn talent.

The best insight to be gleaned of her childhood demeanor is a newspaper column found in a Winnipeg newspaper of the 1940s: the following is part of a column titled "HERE, THERE, and HOLLYWOOD," by entertainment columnist Frank Morris in the *Winnipeg Free Press*, May 27 1946, on his memories of childhood in Winnipeg:

"Oh, those never-to-be-forgotten days on a Winnipeg summer when we used to take over somebody's garage or backyard and put on a performance. We were producers, actors and playwrights all mixed together in one brattish ball of vigor. But the memory of backyard shows that remains with me the strongest is the time we had a guest performer. She was a member of the Winnipeg

Kiddies, an organization that many of you will remember. It was very popular, and the Kiddies toured Canada. Well, this seasoned professional brat turned up for our enactment of a minstrel show. She seated herself on a box and sniffed loudly and derisively at our attempts to put over songs, dances and funny sayings. And so, with more anger than discretion we told her to go ahead and see if she could do better. She took us at our word and thereupon the backyard echoed with her bright, piping little voice, and she kept us in reluctant stitches. None of us had the nerve to finish the show after that, and the little girl went home. Her name was Marjorie Guthrie, and later on we heard that she had left Winnipeg with a girl called Thelma Wolpa, and they were being billed as the White Sisters. Then Marjorie White, with her husband, toured Vaudeville in a very successful act. So successful, as a matter of fact, that Hollywood beckoned, and she turned up with Janet Gaynor and Charles Farrell in one of the first all-musical films, Sunny Side Up. She had a successful movie career being a forerunner of such uninhibited comediennes as Martha Raye and Betty Hutton. Marjorie was killed in an automobile accident. And I never think of her without recalling the wonderful show she put on for us in a Winnipeg backyard."

Behold (on the opposite page) the earliest known "publicity" photos of Marjorie: on the left at age eleven, printed in the *Manitoba Free Press* on November 13, 1915, and on the right, age twelve, in the *Manitoba Free Press* on March 17, 1916.

LITTLE MARJORIE GUTHRIE,
Who will continue singing every afternoon at 3 and 4:30 at the Province, commencing Monday, Nov. 22.

POPULAR LITTLE
ACTRESS ON TOUR

MARJORIE GUTHRIE.

Little Marjorie Guthrie will not be heard in Winnipeg for quite a while. That young lady has set out for a tour in the Aldric circuit of theatres in Western Canada before crossing over to the United States at a big salary.

Dominion fans will remember her acting and singing in "Uncle Tom's Cabin" at the theatre last Christmas in the part of Little Eva, as the Prince in "Cameo Kirby," and as

Her sister,
Belva Harmony Guthrie
1915-1969

Belva, born in 1915, was the baby of the family. She, along with brother Morley, also performed with the Winnipeg Kiddies, following in Marjorie's footsteps. At some point in the 1920s, the family, minus father Robert, moved from Winnipeg to Toronto (he died in Winnipeg in 1937) and for some remaining years, lived at 338 George Street. While growing up there, Belva attended George Street Public School, the same school, incidentally, attended many years earlier by actress Mary Pickford in her youth. She had a measure of notable talent, but in a different vein from older sister Marjorie, for Belva was a singer and musician. This, according to an article in the *Toronto Star*, August 1930, which shows she was active in the performing field early on. As you read this, keep in mind that, factually, it might be completely off the mark, as the publicity machines of those early days had a penchant for hyperbole:

Belva White, 15-year-old sister of Marjorie White, was summoned to Hollywood last Wednesday and yesterday confirmation came to her mother, Mrs. R. Guthrie, 338 George Street, that she had signed a contract with Fox Films. George Street Public School gave Mary Pickford to Hollywood, and now it has given Belva White. Belva is an accomplished singer and pianist. She has been studying with madam DeMonterey. Belva was a member of a kiddies' troupe which traveled from coast to coast and is no stranger to the glamour of footlights and spotlights. Marjorie, whose work in "Sunny Side Up" and other pictures brought her to the fore, telephoned her mother a week ago and asked her to put Belva on the first train to Hollywood. Belva was at that time in Muskoka and it was two days before she could leave Toronto.

She did go on to reasonable popularity of her own in the 1930s, and possibly beyond. Another article, in a society column of the *Star,* says *"Belva White, local gal (or pal) and sister to Marjorie White of the movies is now singing in a cabaret in Syracuse."*

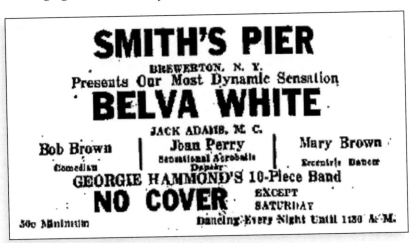

And again, in 1936, she was a local performing star of radio station CKCL, Toronto. Per SSN information, she lived the remainder of her life in New York City, New York, and died there in 1969, at age fifty-four.

Jackie Finesilver, Lillian Beck, Fred Holmes, Catherine Cummings, Gordon Holmes, Margorie Guthrie, Sterling Holmes, Florence Simpson.

The Winnipeg Kiddies

This excerpt from a 1992 newsletter of DANCE COLLECTION DANSE of Toronto, an organization dedicated to preserving the history of dance theater in Canada, is from a piece entitled "THOSE WINNIPEG KIDDIES, 1915-1922":

Founded in 1915 by a Winnipeg accountant named H.A. Smith, a group of child performers first called the 'Returned Soldiers' Association Juvenile entertainers', soon became the famous touring group *Those Winnipeg Kiddies*. The troupe toured Canada and the U.S. by train with a private chef, a piano and a bag of toys. Businessmen in Duluth paid $100 a seat to see them, and in less than one year during WW1 they raised $20,000 for Allied recruiting. Five hundred people had to be turned away because of sold-out notices posted in Fargo North Dakota. The Kiddies gave an extra matinee so as not to disappoint them. Audiences cheered wildly when the Kiddies handed over their Christmas presents to orphans of war heroes.

The Kiddies, directed by Winnipeg's Mrs. R.G. Holmes (seen here at right), were the envy of almost every child in Canada and they thrilled dewy-eyed audiences from Victoria to Toronto and throughout the northern U.S. The group included musicians, singers, dancers, and actors, and though most of them were under 13, they were professionals–their parents were paid $35 a week. Some of the principal performers received $100 per week. They toured with  all expenses paid, stayed in the best hotels and were accompanied by their own traveling teachers. In 1922 little Florence Simpson received roses, a telegram and this fan letter from an admirer: "When I sat in the Orpheum

MARJORIE GUTHRIE

Theater (row 6, seat 15) and gazed into your fair face I was entranced by your sweet voice and your dazzling beauty. I can't eat, I can't see, I can't do a blooming thing." The group disbanded after WWI, but re-formed again in 1919 and toured until their final performance in 1922. But their name lived on with several small troupes taking the title. As late as 1930 the child performers were calling themselves the Winniopeg Kiddies. Some

FAMOUS TROUPE—Here are the original Winnipeg Kiddies as they appeared during the height of their fame during the last war. At the top is Marjorie Guthrie, who later achieved fame in the movies as Marjorie White. She died a few years ago of injuries received in an auto accident. From left to right those standing are: Gordon Holmes, Jackie Finesilver, Lillian Beck, Violet Budd, Alberta Smith, Walter Hall and Fred Holmes.

of the original Kiddies continued their performing careers in Canada, the U.S., and England. "In looking through some early photos, former Kiddies' director, Mrs. Holmes said, 'It is so long ago, and daresay the photographs make us all look very quaint. But they were lovely children, those Winnipeg Kiddies'." David Taylor provided another clue which led DCD to Brenda DaFoe, the daughter of "little" Florence Simpson. Three weeks later, Brenda provided the CBC (Canada Broadcasting Corporation) with an interview, and sang, for all entranced listeners, the song which her mother sang with the Kiddies — 'The Girl in the Alice Blue Gown.'

Writer Margaret Kennedy penned a feature article entitled "Where Are the Winnipeg Kiddies?" in the *Winnipeg Free Press* on September 14, 1940. While not entirely factually accurate, it *does* show how memories of the Kiddies troupe from so many years before had stayed fresh and alive in many peoples' minds and hearts:

> "Star and queen of the group, as well as its oldest member, Marjorie Guthrie, was the center of every tableau. Her Blond curls bobbed and her blue eyes twinkled as she sang and danced her way into the heart of every child, man and woman who saw her. Marjorie was 15 (?) when she joined the "Kiddies" and after three years of touring with them, she left for the brighter stages of new York. Dorothy McKay was taken into the company to replace the enchanting "Queen." After Marjorie became settled in New York, she sent for Thelma Wolpa, another member of the troupe, and the two became known as the "White Sisters," touring successfully for some years on the old Keith Vaudeville circuit. Marjorie married Eddie Tierney, of song and dance fame, and then she and Thelma tried their luck in Hollywood. Marjorie White soon became a contract player with M.G.M., played bits in minor pictures, did an excellent portrayal of a small part in Possessed, which starred Joan Crawford and Clark Gable. She advanced to a minor role in The Golden Calf, but will be best remembered for her gaiety in Sunny Side Up, with Janet Gaynor. While still under contract to Metro Goldwyn Mayer, she died tragically in an automobile accident near Hollywood in 1935. Edan and Florence Simpson had one very spectacular number in the show, supporting Marjorie Guthrie in a beautiful waltz. Pincus Leff [2] originally from St. Paul, returned to that city when the troupe broke up. Then there were John Simpson, Morley Guthrie, younger brother of Marjorie, Cissie Farnsworth, and Grace Gilmore, all at one time on the road with the Kiddies, and who appear to have passed into obscurity.

Note: I have in my collection a series of over forty pictures and newspaper clippings from the scrapbook of Edna Patrick, on loan to the DCD by Ms. Patrick's granddaughter, for the purpose of making an electronic record of them. Many thanks to Ms. Amy Bowring of the DCD staff for making them available for use in this biography.

Fred Stone
1873-1959

Fred Stone is a pivotal figure in this piece because he was instrumental in steering Marjorie into show business and a performing career. An itinerant circus acrobat, rodeo clown, and other assorted performing stints, later a stage and film actor, as well as producer/director, he saw Marjorie at a community performance in Winnipeg, and introduced her to the newly formed Winnipeg Kiddies troupe. It was he, also, who brought the two shows "Tip-Top" and "Topsy and Eva" to the stage on both coasts, both of which originally starred the Duncan Sisters, who in both works were later replaced by the White Sisters. His best known early work was as the scarecrow in the 1902-1911 stage production of *The Wizard of Oz*. He was also an avid rodeo fan, and toured with his buddy Will Rogers with a semi-comedy "ridin & ropin" act across the U.S. and Canada in the early years of the century. It was during one of these tours they played Winnipeg about 1915, when he first met Marjorie. But even earlier, he co-highlighted a duo song & dance comedy act with David Montgomery (naturally known as "Montgomery & Stone"). Their best known act was a Victor Herbert piece titled *The Red Mill* (1906). Among the very earliest of pre-Vaudeville comics, Stone was passé and pretty much forgotten even in the heyday years of Vaudeville, the 1920s, although he did continue his stage and film work up into the 1950s.

His autobiography, *Rolling Stone*, was published in New York in 1945, and a biography, *Fred Stone*, published by author Armond Fields in 2002.

Stone appeared in two films in current television release, which can be seen on TCM frequently: *Alice Adams* (1935), starring Katherine Hepburn, and *The Westerner* (1940), starring Gary Cooper.

*Fred Stone's autobiography, published
1945.*

The White Sisters

Thelma Wolpa's mother figures prominently in the formation of The White Sisters as a team. It was during the 1910s that Thelma's father, an itinerant newssheet salesman who was always on the road, had an opportunity for money-making that took him to Winnipeg, Canada. Mother Myrtle, the typical domineering "stage mother," with Thelma in tow, followed him there, and introduced Thelma to the Kiddies troupe. It was here she met young Marjorie, and from the very start the two girls "clicked" together as friends and duo performers. Not long after, Thelma's father again re-located to San Francisco, and again mother and daughter followed. Myrtle did her best to find show-biz work for her daughter, mostly with only minor success. Remembering how Thelma and Marjorie had done so well together with the Kiddies in Canada, she contacted the Guthries in Winnipeg, asking for Marjorie to join them in California.

Marjorie's train trip to San Francisco could have taken several different routes. I've been unable to determine her exact point-of-entry, and since Minneapolis is due south of Winnipeg, she could have traveled there, switched trains westward to Seattle, and then south to San Francisco. This would be the longer of the two, involving changing three different trains. Or, let's assume she went straight from Winnipeg to Vancouver/Seattle, transferred there to a U.S. train, and south to San Francisco, involving only two trains. But this remains a detail we'll never know. Several previous biographies tell of her going first to New York and sending for Thelma to join here there. But immigration records show her first point-of-arrival as San Francisco, on December 21, 1921 (what would she have been doing, all alone, at age 17, in New York?). I hope this lays that rumor to rest.

Marjorie did, indeed, arrive in San Francisco on December 21, 1921, to live with them at 482 Haight Street (this area, Haight-Ashbury, was a haven for Bohemians and artistic types long before the hippie era of the 1960s), and tried to find work wherever they could. By dint of perseverance, mother contacted Bert Levy, a big-time agent on the coast, and the two girls auditioned for him. He liked them, and booked them into a San Francisco playhouse called The Butterfield. Audiences loved them, and they became known as "Wolpa and Guthrie, Little Bits of Everything." This was the first real public performance act by the two, with Marjorie in a Scottish costume doing the Highland Fling, and Thelma in Russian costume doing "Stars And Stripes forever." Their duo piece was a comedy number called "On the Bowery," in which Thelma played the boy, Marjorie the girl. After a number of other small-time gigs at various theaters and playhouses in the Bay Area, with Thelma's mom always looking to get her girls better bookings, Myrtle decided to take the two to New York. Along the way, they played their way across the country, spending two weeks in Kansas City doing a number called "Pretty Baby," before moving on to New York. Once there, they led a hardscrabble existence, until mother took them to see Harry Fitzgerald, a big-time agent of New York (he handled a number of acts, including Milton Berle and Baby Rose Marie). He put them on the bill, unpaid, at a dinner function attended by a large number of New York agents.

But, how did Marj and Thelma became known as "The White Sisters"? The following passage is quoted verbatim from pages 25 and 26 of Thelma's book:

> "When it came time for us, the emcee asked who we were. "Wolpa and Guthrie, Little Bits of Everything," screamed mother in his ear. "Whaddysay?" wheezed the emcee, puffing a big cigar in her face. "The girl in the black dress Marjorie Guthrie," shrieked mother in his ear, "The one in white is Thelma Wolpa." "Ooooh" nodded the emcee. "I get it. Black one Marjorie…white one…Thelma." Before mother could say anything more, he staggered out on the stage. "Ladeez and gennulmen, now we present, direct from…er…well, here they are…the famous… er…Thelma….White…and…er…LADEEZ AND GENNULMEN, THE WHITE SISTERS."

That night the White Sisters were born. The next morning, mother got a telegram from Max Hayes, one of the biggest agents in New York. He wanted to see them right away. He had seen them in their performance the night before, and was quite impressed with them. He booked them into the 14th Street Follies, a neighborhood theater known as one of the toughest houses in the city. When mother questioned him, he replied, "Yes, it's the toughest theater in New York, but you know the old saying,

'If they like you at the Follies, they'll love you anywhere else.'" The crowd went wild at their act, and that was all Max Hayes needed.

They had passed the 14th Street crowd, and the White sisters were on their way. Within a week, mother had signed them to a five-year contract with the B.F. Keith Vaudeville circuit, and were known by such alliterative sobriquets as "The White Sisters, Braodway's Brightest Little

The lobby of the Palace Theater, at 1564 Braodway.

Stars," "New Twinklers In Stardom," and a dozen or so more. By this time Loews, the Pantages and Gus Edwards were all clamoring for them. They had finally reached the ultimate when they were booked into the Palace Theater, at 15th and Broadway, one of the most prestigious houses in all of New York. In the following year, they appeared there ten more times, a record that has never been equaled.

After a few months of headlining Broadway, they got a call from none other than impresario Flo Ziegfeld himself. He wanted them in a show he was putting together at the Amsterdam, on 43rd Street, to be called "The Ziegfeld Frolics." They found themselves among some of the top names in show business, notably Will Rogers, and Bill Robinson. [3] When the "Frolics" finally closed, they headed back to the West Coast in the road show *Tip-Top*, a short stint in San Francisco with that number, then down to Los Angeles to replace the Duncan Sisters in *Topsy and Eva* at the Alcazar. Marjorie played the role of Topsy, Thelma played Eva. But that gig didn't last long, it closed after only a short run, and the three of them headed back to New York once again to the world of Vaudeville.

By this time, they were already well-known, and mother had no trouble finding bookings for the two. They were now in big time, making more money than ever: mother bought them expensive wardrobes, even a car with a hired chauffeur to ferry them around. But after two years of the high life in New York, they were once again booked for another cross-country tour. They did short stints at the Keith House in Boston, two weeks at Cleveland's Orpheum, Los Angeles again, a few months in St. Louis, the Majestic in Fort Worth, and a score of others. Then back to New York. The two were quite busy with all the road shows and endless traveling, finally ending up back in New York working the Keith circuit. According to Thelma's memoirs, during this period personal and professional matters became more and more pressing, and they parted company as performers. The White Sisters were no more, even though both of them continued using the stage name "White" to the end of their lives and remained close friends. Quite an auspicious career, those few short years between 1922 and 1925.

In the later years of her life Thelma found work as a business agent for several notable show business celebrities, including James Coburn, Robert Blake, and others.

The fact that their names are still well-known today speaks highly of their talent and popularity. At the time they parted ways, Marjorie was but 21, Thelma a mere 15. There are no recordings of their voices, and unless someone, somewhere, has a spool of nitrate film produced by a hand-cranked camera of their performance, we'll never really know just how good they really were. *Ah, but wasn't that a time!*

The Duncan Sisters

Evelyn Duncan 1893-1972

Evelyn, the older sister of Rosetta and Vivian, did more behind-the-scenes work, such as writing and producing their acts, and rarely actually played on stage with them. She was to them, work-wise and business-wise, what Moe Howard was to the Three Stooges (no pun intended).

Vivian Duncan 1897-1986

Composer, songwriter, and entertainer of the Duncan sisters, Vivian played Eva in the Broadway musical *Topsy and Eva*, for which she and her sister Rosetta wrote the music. With her sister, she also appeared in *Doing Our Bit, She's a Good Fellow, Tip-Top*, and other Vaudeville works.

Joining ASCAP in 1942, Vivian's other popular compositions include "Do-Re-Mi," "I Never Had A Mammy," "The Moon Am Shinin'," "Someday Soon," "Los Angeles," "Hollywood Belongs To The World," and "United We Stand."

Rosetta Duncan 1894-1959

She played Topsy in the musical *Topsy and Eva* for which she helped write the music with her sister Vivian. She also appeared in *Doing Our Bit, She's a Good Fellow,* and *Tip-Top.* The Duncan Sisters had a long and illustrious career, and continued performing until the late 1950s. The only connection they had with the White Sisters are the two plays *Tip-Top* and *Topsy and Eva,* both of which premiered with the Duncans, who were replaced by the Whites at some point during the runs of those shows. They made a film version of their act for United Artists in 1927. There is no indication that the two acts ever met each other. Another connection is a bit more personal: My mother remembers seeing the Duncans on stage in Chicago as a young girl in the 1930s.

PICKWICK ARMS HOTEL GREENWICH, CONN.
New England's most beautiful family and transient hotel. Twenty-eight miles from New York.
Open all year. Under ownership-management.

The Pickwick Arms Hotel in Greenwich, Connecticut, where Marjorie and Eddie were married on August 10, 1924.

Marjorie & Eddie

Early in 1924, the White Sisters were playing the Orpheum, in Los Angeles, when on the same bill with them was a handsome young performer named Eddie Tierney. He and Marjorie took quite a liking to each other almost immediately, and began seeing each other more and more (Marjorie coming in later and later each night, to the consternation of Thelma's mother). Not long after, she boldly announced that they were in love, and would soon be married. At this point, it gets a bit hard to determine where they were at any given time. Early in the year they were in Los Angeles and in August 1924 they married in Connecticut, and were soon once again headed back to the West Coast. It would appear that Marjorie and Eddie's marriage signaled the beginning of the end of the White Sisters as a team. Although they continued to perform together, each was going in her own direction in show business, but they remained close friends for the rest of her life. Marjorie and Eddie performed on stage together in a number of light productions, the most noted of which, and reviewed in several papers and journals, was a skit called "GWAFUS, GWAFUS, GWAFUS." This ridiculous comedy played at the Orpheum in 1926, presumably in San Francisco or Oakland (today, there exists no reference to this work in New York).

Marjorie and Eddie were married at the Pickwick Arms Hotel, in Greenwich, Connecticut, on August 10, 1924. *The New York Times* article of August 11 read as follows:

> "Miss Marjorie Gutherie, known on the stage as Miss Marjorie White, of the White Sisters of Vaudeville, was married to Edwin J. Tierney at the Pickwick Arms, Greenwich, this afternoon at 2 o'clock. The ceremony was performed under one of the arbors on the front lawn by Justice of The Peace William S. Fiske in the presence of a large party of friends from New York, including a number of prominent actors and actresses. Mr. Tierney is in the

musical comedy 'Keep Kool' at the Globe Theater, New York, a member of the dancing team of Tierney and Donnelly. Johnny Dooley, who is playing the lead comedy role in the same play, and his wife, acted as best man and matron of honor. The bride is a native of Canada." (Their marriage license shows his occupation as "Dance Instructor.")

This is the only photo I have of the two of them together, at their home, 8228 Sunset Boulevard:

Eddie Tierney

Other than demographic information on his birth in 1898, and New York Census records of his family, I could find little, if anything, looking for Marj's husband Eddie Tierney. There was another actor named Edward Tierney, born in 1928, but he was no relation, and he was not related at all to the more famous Tierneys, Gene and Lawrance.

There's nothing in print on their relationship during their marriage, or what he was really like, the kind of man and husband he was. But the information that does survive does not exactly portray him as a very nice guy, to say the least. The only public photos of him appear in the *Los Angeles Times*, marking his presence at the Coroner Inquest of her death in 1935. From the scant info I have, it seems that as her career was rising, his was beginning to "go down the tubes," and quickly. He did do some stage work, early on, and during their marriage; yet he would take umbrage at being called "Mister White."

In the years after her passing, the last news of him is from 1943, noting the second divorce from his second wife (married and divorced the same woman twice). Tierney was arrested on a charge of arson in 1938 for setting his wife's apartment on fire, and was again nabbed in 1938 sentenced to 90 days in the Monterey County Jail for passing bad checks. A January 1936 *Los Angeles Times and Herald Examiner* article detailed his first divorce from his second wife, Marie Riker. Stay with me here: she sued for annulment after having been married only a month or so, claiming she was too drunk at the time to realize what she was doing. They were married in December 1935, only a few short months after Marjorie's passing. After the 1943 divorce article, he seems to have disappeared off the face of the earth: rumor has it that he died in 1959 or 1960.

Marjorie on Stage

Hello, Lola

Eltinge 42nd Street Theatre (1/12/1926-circa. 2/19/26)
Maxine Elliott's Theatre (2/8/1926-2/20/1926)

Category: Musical, Comedy, Original, Broadway
Description: A musical in three acts
Setting: The Baxter home and the Parcher home

Hello Lola, a musical rendition, produced by the Schuberts, of Booth Tarkington's *Seventeen*, played at the Eltinge on West 42nd Street, and Maxine Elliot's on West 39th Street, for 47 performances in January and February 1926, with Marjorie in the role of Jane Baxter. This is her first known work, solo, on the legitimate stage. An earlier version, under the original Tarkington title, played at the Booth Theater on West 45th Street, starring Ruth Gordon, and featuring Lillian Ross in the Jane Baxter role.

There exist several newspaper pieces, during that same month, on a skit with Marjorie and husband Eddie called *Gwafus, Gwafus, Gwafus* at San Francisco's Orpheum. There doesn't seem to be any more on this show beyond the brief clips in the *Oakland Tribune,* and there is no record at all of the piece on the East Coast.

Top: The Eltinge Theater 245 West 42nd Street, Circa 1912.

Bottom: Maxine Elliot's Theater (later CBS Studio 51), 101 West 38th Street.

Ballet Moderne

Gallo Opera House, (4/9/1928-4/21/1928)

Category: Special, Ballet, Revue, Original, Broadway
Description: A ballet revue in two parts

This, her second legitimate work, played only 14 performances at the Gallo Opera House, 254 West 54th Street, much later known as the famous (or infamous) Studio 54. The Gallo was a true opera house, not a theater as we know. Little is known of *Ballet Moderne*, other than the fact that it was a serious operatic work, a real high-brow, long-hair piece, by a Russian composer, Gavrilov.

The Gallo House, 254 West 54th Street.

If Marjorie did appear in this one, it's doubtful if she has a character name at all. Program listings show such luminaries as Jascha Heifitz, Sergei Prokofiev, and others of that ilk, far removed from Vaudeville and comedy, way, way up at the top end of the scale.

Why was Marjorie in this one at all? We'll never know. In all the program information about this show, her name is mentioned only once, and that in the one-paragraph review in Billboard magazine. Maybe she tried it to see if she could do this "really legit" stuff or not: most likely discovered she couldn't, or didn't like it, and never tried it again.

Lady Fingers

Vanderbilt Theatre, (1/31/1929-circa. 3/1929)
Liberty Theatre, (4/1/1929-5/25/1929)

Category: Musical, Comedy, Original, Broadway
Description: A musical in two acts
*Setting: Pennsylvania Station, New York; En route; Dr. Jasper's Health
Farm*

Lady Fingers was a remake of an earlier work *Easy Come Easy Go,*
written and produced by Eddie Buzzell, and featured Marjorie as Molly
Maloney and Buzzell as Jim Bailey.

Buzzell did the rewrite himself, and hand-picked Marjorie for the
Nurse Molly role. As luck would provide, Fox Studios' executive Winfield Sheehan caught her act and immediately signed her to Fox to play
in *Sunny Side Up.*

On the top of the facing page we see a scene from *Lady Fingers,* with
Eddie Buzzell left, Marjorie right as Nurse Molly, and John Price Jones,
center. The play drew rave reviews throughout the community and made
her a top favorite among stage comediennes.

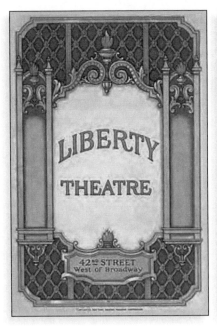

This photo shows Marjorie on stage as Molly Maloney, with fellow performer Jim Diamond as character Shadow Martin in Lady Fingers.

The photo on this page shows her in "civilian" pose, sans makeup or image.[4] Such photos were standard test shots taken of a new studio employee for purposes of study to see how they would look for makeup, wardrobe, camera angles, etc. Compare this one with the previous picture of her on stage with actor Diamond in the play *Ladyfingers:* considering the dates of both the play and the release of *Sunny Side Up,* and it would appear both photos were taken within a very short time of each other.

Hot-Cha (Laid in Mexico)

Ziegfeld Theatre, (3/8/1932-6/18/1932)

Category: Musical, Comedy, Original, Broadway
Description: A musical in two acts
Setting: New York and Mexico City

By 1932, having established herself as a true up-and-comer on the stage and screen with the resounding success of *Sunny Side Up* and *Happy Days*, followed by a handful of lesser films, the Great Depession was taking hold. Marjorie's "good-time-cutesy-little-flapper" image was becoming passé and beginning to wear thin. Audiences were now more interested in "escapist-fantasy" works a la Busby Berkeley musicals like *42nd Street* and the "Golddigger" films. In that year, no film work came her way. However, Marjorie's perseverance kept her working, mainly by personal appearances and assorted Vaudeville-type acts. It was Flo Ziegfeld who came to her rescue and helped to re-introduce her to the public by signing her to a truly top-of-the-line production, *Hot-Cha (Laid in Mexico)*. Headlined by such luminaries as Bert Lahr, Lupe Velez, Charles "Buddy" Rogers and others, Marjorie played the role of Toodles Smith, at Ziegeld's own theater situated at 6th Avenue and 54th Street: this was big-time Broadway, to say the least. Although her part was small,

amounting to not much more than a few cameo walk-ons, she knew from experience how to make her presence known, and the audience came to remember her as the *real* star of the show.

The Ziegfeld, at 6th Avenue at 54th Street.

Marjorie: Movie Star

Sunny Side Up (1929)

Marjorie was contacted by Winnie Sheehan in May 1929 for this film. The date would indicate the signing took place either while *Lady Fingers* was still running, or immediately after its closing, May 25, 1929. This would give her a substantial presence of character. For her screen debut, she played second to lead Janet Gaynor, as opposed to the one-scene walk-ons she was used to in her stage work. As character Bea Nichols she filled the spot perfectly. The story itself was promoted as a light musical, and, yes, it was Gaynor who sang most of the numbers (quite admirably at that), but without Marjorie at her side, Janet would have been hard-pressed to flesh out her role. With Gaynor, admittedly, the better actress, it was Marjorie who proved herself as the consummate entertainer. Her joie de vie and natural élan shine through above the others: she's the real star. One could say that what Garbo was to drama, and Jean Harlow to sex appeal, Marjorie was to comic entertainment. All in all, an eminently pleasurable film to watch.

Happy Days (1929)

Originally titled "The New Orleans Frolic," this was one of several Fox productions that went through the name-changing process during that period of confusion caused by the frenzy surrounding the dawn of sound in film. But in its final release, version *Happy Days* [5] provided Marjorie, in her character of Margie, as the keystone figure of the story to Will Rogers, George Jessel, Warner Baxter, among other stellar stars in the film. Janet Gaynor and Charles Farrell also appear, but not in the forefront as they did in *Sunny Side Up*. For the second consecutive time Marjorie's is a center-stage role, rather than a second unit walk-on part. But beyond her appearance, the story becomes rather disjointed and falls apart into a massive choral display highlighting a mélange of celebrities.

New Movietone Follies of 1930
(A.K.A. Svenson's Wild Party)

This book is attempting to avoid technical specifics on these works, and rather concentrate on Marjorie, but in this case an exception must be made. All we know of her character is the name, Vera Fontaine. Here Marjorie appears in the company of Noel Francis, Miriam Seegar, and Frank Richardson, and of course, the ubiquitous El Brendel.

The reason for the separate titles can be found on page 187 of the book *A Song in the Dark: The Birth of the Musical Film* by Richard Barrios (Oxford University Press, 1995): in a nutshell, it had much to do with the adverse economics of the Great Depression. In order to recoup their investment, Fox distributed the film to the widest of possible audiences. The following is an excerpt from Barrios' explanation of Fox's marketing strategy:

From an unknown fan magazine, early 1930.

*"Fox did its best to sell the picture as anything other than a revue.
'Follies' in the title seemed a dead giveaway, and after considering
re-naming it 'Movietonia,' the company played to Brendel's comedic
strength. The Follies played San Francisco as 'Svenson's Wild Party'
and in Minneapolis whose Scandinavian community loved Brendel,
as 'Svenson's Night Out'"* [6]

*Two newspaper ads — same film — two titles (notice two more "losties": In
the left ad* Voice of Hollywood *and on the right* Her Golden Calf).

Just Imagine (1930)

I'll capsulize this by stating that I'm a biographer, not a film critic, so I'll try not to go into too much detail describing this Z-grade atrocity of 1930 sci-fi fantasy that even Marjorie White couldn't save, through her character "D-6." It *did*, though, make a name for a few top-grade actors such as Frank Albertson, John Garrick, Maureen O'Sullivan and a bevy of others, and welcomed back such classic veteran actors Hobart Bosworth, Mischa Auer, and, oh yes, the forever-abysmal El Brendel.[6] A few song-and-dance numbers featuring Marjorie and Frank Albertson are the only scenes worth watching in this one.

Oh, For a Man (1930)

Another step down for Marjorie into a one-scene extra part: her character Totsy Franklin doesn't appear until almost an hour into the film, and she's relegated to a minor secondary part as the wife of one of Reginald Denny's friends, nothing more. She does, however, sing one tune: "I'm Just Nuts About You."

Oh, For a Man was based on a story called "Stolen Thunder," written by Mary Watkins, which was published in the *Saturday Evening Post*, June 1930 (this information thanks to Eleanor Knowles Dugan, owner of *www.jeanetteandnelson.net*).

Charlie Chan Carries On (1931)

A still (opposite page) and three lobby cards are the only photos of Marjorie I've been able to find on this film, a true rarity. That's her at the very front, left side. While posters and other materials are in abundance, the only known existing copies of the film itself rest in the George Eastman House and The Library of Congress.

However, in 2005, a copy ran at one of the Stanford University theaters, so apparently there's at least one copy in someone's private collection, somewhere.

Marjorie's character in this one is named Sadie Minchinher, the wife of a socialite involved in the mystery, but the film's importance lies in the fact that it is the very first in the long series of Chan films, this one starring Warner Oland. A complete full print of the entire working script of this film, as well as several others, can be found at *www.charliechanfamily.com*, an excellent website for Chan fans.

The Lost Films
Hollywood Halfbacks (1931)

For *Hollywood Halfbacks* the Internet Movie Database (IMDb) has a sketchy listing for the title, with Marjorie in the cast (along with Vernon Dent), but with no character name. Produced by Universal, the only known copy rests in The Library of Congress. No other information can be found.

Her Bodyguard (1933)

Her Bodyguard, filmed by Paramount, is another lost work. IMDb has her character shown as "Lita," but nothing else is known about this one. Neither Eastman House nor The Library of Congress has any record. The only synopsis I could find was *Fandango.com*, quoted here: "When the actress girlfriend of a rich man is pursued by a producer, the rich man hires bodyguard Lowe (Edward) to protect her, but Lowe falls in love with her, too *(All Movie Guide)*." It's also rumored that a nitrate print of the film exists in the UCLA Film and Television Archives, with Universal as owner to the rights. *IT'S ALIVE! IT'S ALIVE! I'VE FOUND IT! AND IT SUCKS!!*

Her Golden Calf (1930)

Her Golden Calf is *truly* an oddity: the existing copies of the title, for sale widely on eBay and Amazon, is a Soviet-made epic of the same era, over three hours long, un-translated, no subtitles, copyrighted circa 1968, even re-formatted from PAL to NTSC for sale in the West. All advertising describe the American version in its entirety, but this is *not the same film at all.* Another version of the same title is currently available, and which several collectors, myself included, were duped into buying: this version is a religious-themed tale geared to children. So be careful when considering this one: *neither* of the two is the original film. Per the *New York Times'* plot description, Marjorie's character is named Alice, and the story is about life in New York's Greenwich Village and Coney Island — allegedly a comedy. The only semi-complete synopsis found was again on Fandango.com, here in its entirety:

> In this pygmalionesque musical a drab secretary leads a boring life until a good friend intervenes. The friend begins a total make-over upon her friend. First she slathers her in mud packs, and then she encases her in lovely silk dresses. Soon the plain woman is transformed into an extraordinary beauty. It is no surprise that her boss, not knowing her true identity, falls hopelessly in love with her. Singing, dancing and romancing ensues. Songs include "A Picture No Artist Can Paint," "You Gotta Be Modernistic," "I'm Telling The World About You," "Maybe Someday," and "I Can't Help It" *(Sandra Brennan, All Movie Guide).*

The most complete contemporary storyline to be found was a review in the *Toronto Star*, which tells of the main character (Jack Mulhall) a dance director, putting on a cheesecake show, searching for the "golden calf" (as in women's legs) looking for that perfect "gam" to use in his upcoming production.

A few other lost motion pictures that *might* feature White include *Voice of Hollywood #11 Second Series* (1930). Marjorie was allegedly uncredited in this one, but no known copies exist. The same is true for *Sob Sister* (1931), in which she has been rumored to have been cast, but no record exists to verify this. A little-known fact about *Sob Sister* which may have given birth to the rumor was that the DeSilva, Brown, and Henderson tune "If I Had a Talking Picture of You" from *Sunny Side Up* was apparently also used in *Sob Sister*; again, no known copies exist to verify or dispel the rumor.

The March of Time (1930)
Broadway to Hollywood (1933)

The March of Time and *Broadway to Hollywood* are a bit more detailed as to their origins (and demise) than the others in this category, and great insight on these films can be gleaned from the aforementioned Barrios book. *March of Time* was to be MGM's counterpoint of Fox's "Movietone Follies" series. However, MGM, whose executives' judgment of public acceptance (as well as more astute number-crunchers) realized that the genre had by that time worn out its welcome. This one was a disaster-in-the-making which could quite well have bankrupted them. Part way through the production they scrapped the project wholesale, but kept the dailies and used footage for possible use in a future film. Indeed, three years later, the cuts were used in *Broadway to Hollywood*, another fiasco due to its terrible makeup. Scenes and takes were patched together, unrelated to each other, with no continuity whatsoever, a hodge-podge mess with no discernable plot or storyline anywhere. Both works featured a bevy of performers of the day, including Bing Crosby, The Duncan Sisters, Buster Keaton, Betty Healy (Ted's wife), Ramon Navarro, Marie Dressler, Alice Brady, Madge Evans, Mickey Rooney, Jimmy Durante, Nelson Eddy, Moe and Curly Howard, among others. The credits even list a piece with Albertina Rasch and her dancers, but not used (too bad — the Rasch dancers were a creditable act, albeit a primitive precursor to Busby Berkely's choreography and the legendary Rockettes). Even though both films are truly gone, rumor persists that a copy of *Broadway to Hollywood* is out there somewhere.

One other film that Marjorie White is rumored to have appeared in is Wheeler and Woolsey's RKO vehicle *Girl Crazy* (1932), but nothing exists to affirm or deny whether Marjorie was included but cut, signed but not used, or worked in this one at all.

The 1930s

These two years were a very busy time for Marjorie. In addition to all her travels and personal appearances, she worked in six films in 1931, at four different studios: *Charlie Chan Carries On, Women of All Nations,* and *The Black Camel* at Fox, *Broadminded* at Warner Bros., *Hollywood Halfbacks* at Universal and, the biggest one of all *Possessed* alongside Joan Crawford and Clark Gable at MGM.

Now that her name had been firmly established, Marjorie was on a roll, but seemingly in search of a "home" where her talents could be best put to use. In the midst of her film work she found enough time for herself to enjoy life. April 1930 saw an addition to her family, a nephew born in Toronto.[7] In August 1931, she spent a weekend with friends at Catalina Island, a hour by speed boat from Los Angeles.

A tidbit from a *Los Angeles Times* celebrity column made mention of the Bird Park jaunt and told of her heroic efforts, with the others, to bale water out of the boat that had sprung a leak. In December 1930, she was in Toronto once again, visiting her mother, sister, and other family.

An interesting find: *The Toronto Star,* August 6, 1930, boasts an article stating that Belva, then age 15, had taken the name "White" and gone to Hollywood to work with her sister. (See Belva's chapter for more on this.)

On the road again less than two weeks later, after a visit to New York, Marjorie was in Philadelphia with husband Eddie. They were in a taxi traveling from their stay at the Warwick Hotel en route to the studios of radio station WPEN for an interview when calamity struck. Their taxi was involved in a serious accident, and Marjorie suffered several broken ribs and bruises. It is unknown whether she made it to the radio studio at all, given her injuries.

Women of All Nations (1931)

Once again consigned to a cut scene walk-on near the film's beginning, her character PeeWee received no screen credit. Headed up by comedians Arthur McLaglen & Edmund Lowe and their counterparts Fifi D'Orsay and Greta Nissen, the story of Flaff and Quirt is (supposedly) about director Raoul Walsh's memory of two marines he met in WWI. A full synopsis of this story can be found at the websites *tcm.com, imdb.com* and *fandango.com.*

The Black Camel (1931)

With few exceptions, the years 1931 and 1932 were not exactly kind to Marjorie in the roles she played for Fox. In *The Black Camel*, she is in only a couple of scenes, her character Bea Nichols undefined to the others in the story — she's just there, another extra of the crowd. Despite boasting such stars as Warner Oland as Chan, Bela Lugosi as Tarnaverro the psychic, Sally Eilers as the lead female, my personal favorite of the cast (other than Marjorie) would be Dwight Frye. Frye would become famous as Renfield in Universal's *Dracula*, and Fritz in *Frankenstein*.[9] But she *does* give a couple lines that help Chan unravel the mystery.

But as slow as things were going for Marjorie (a big reason she went to Broadway in 1932's *Hot Cha*), things were about to take a turn for the better, and truly catapult her into big-time stardom…

Broadminded (1931)

Having signed a five-year contract with Fox in 1929, Marjorie was by now acutely aware of how her initial splash in *Sunny Side Up* and *Happy Days* had ebbed to almost nothing. She managed to end her employ with Fox and went to Warner Bros in 1931 with her dossier full of her credits, and her reputation on her shoulder. The Warners welcomed her, and at once set to make full use of her potential and starlet quality by casting her as Penny Packer in their big-screen epic *Broadminded*. This was her first grand leap into the true big time. Alongside comic Joe E. Brown, and another up-and-coming sexpot starlet, Thelma Todd, along with a bevy of other already well-established Hollywood names, this time was no hope-for-the-best effort: she was finally on the "A" list of young film starlets. All the years of hard work had finally paid off: the film garnered

unparalleled success at the box office, and Marjorie was now, at last, a real movie star. But, the best was yet to come.

Possessed (1931)

In the company of such luminaries as Clark Gable and Joan Crawford, and under the tutelage of acclaimed director Clarence Brown (famous for his work with Greta Garbo), Marjorie was now among the biggest names of the silver screen in her *Possessed* character Vernice LaVerne. There was no turning back now. Here she stood, in the presence of greatness. Although in this one, as others, she plays only one scene, this one scene was different: her scene is vital to the storyline, and her character (in Marjorie's first try at serious semi-dramatic acting) comes across quite well as the perfect antithesis to the stuffed-shirt "hoi polloi" who fill out the story. And to let us know she's still Marjorie White, she throws in a couple of risque double-entendres to boot. Also featured briefly is Geno Corrado of Three Stooges fame.

Here's an interesting aside on the relationship between Marjorie and Joan Crawford: it has become known that Marjorie was a huge Joan Crawford fan, and here's a copy of a letter Joan sent her thanking her for her admiration (available from from Joan Crawford's website *www. JoanCrawfordBest.com,* under "letters 1930s"). The fact that the two knew each other, if only slightly, and that both were in the same business, Joan already a major star, and Marjorie a struggling young starlet, gives rise to the thought that possibly Joan may have used her insider connections to get Marjorie a job, however small, in a big-money motion picture, if only to help her make ends meet and pay the rent.

The closing line of the letter, "I trust you will find success very soon," belies the fact that Joan knew Marjorie, if only through their work in films, and shows us a glimpse of Joan's warmth and caring.

Diplomaniacs (1933)

After severing her ties with Fox, Marjorie's next six films saw her skipping from company to company: Warners, MGM, Universal, RKO, Paramount and finally Columbia, one picture each, for the remainder of her career.

Diplomaniacs found her at RKO, the "poverty row" cousin of Fox, cast in the role of Dolores aside veteran vaudevillians Wheeler & Woolsey, actress Phyllis Barry, and seasoned old-timers Louis Calhern and Hugh Herbert.

Although I find Wheeler & Woolsey's brand of comedy just dated and absurdly silly, Marjorie's Dolores fits in well in this rendition of vaudeville *shtick*. She's in her domain of comic ingénue, particularly in her song-and-dance routine with Wheeler on the deck of the ship. And she continues on, scene by scene throughout the picture, as opposed to her usual-by-now one-scene walk-ons, as this time her character is integral to the story. The dialogue, done in a crude semi-rhyming fashion, can be viewed as

Diplomaniacs *publicity still with Phyllis Barry (with thanks to Frank R. for this one from his collection).*

a precursor to *Woman Haters*, to come the following year. Yes, she stood out once again in this one, as in most of her other efforts. Regardless of who headed the bill, Marjorie was the real star.

Woman Haters (1934)

Woman Haters is probably the best known and most thoroughly documented of all Marjorie White films, so there is no need to cover its description here. But it *does* remind us of my original question: "Who was she, and whatever became of her?" This idle curiosity led your author on the search for her life and career.

We all know by now that *Woman Haters* was the very first comedy short by The Three Stooges on their own, free of Ted Healy, and was the premier product of Columbia's "musical novelty" genre, formed in the early 1930s as a money-saving tax write-off and a way to recoup their investment in the scores of contract players and capital equipment in the depths of the Great Depression. Company execs like Harry Cohn had little idea that this "shorts" department would not only keep the company financially afloat, but become their biggest money maker over the next twenty years.

At the time of the theatrical release of *Woman Haters* in 1934, the Stooges were a relatively obscure Vaudeville act, using the name "Howard, Fine, and Howard." But Marjorie was an established starlet, a household name to comedy fans for well over a decade. Hence, the marquee placed her name as the lead, with star billing, over the other three. This was the first and *only* time her name topped the bill. In the course of licensing arrangements to Screen Gems Television in the 1950s, the bill was

A publicity still from Woman Haters.

changed to read "The Three Stooges with Marjorie White."The complete
story of how this one was put together can be found on page 78 of Moe
Howard's book, *Moe Howard and the Three Stooges*. Several actresses were
auditioned for the part, but Marjorie was the only one with the right
charisma/persona, nuances of character, and who could hold the timing
just right, she got the part.[10] And added to that she was one of the few

Another publicity still from Woman Haters.

whose name had been familiar to the public for a long time, so the audience knew, going in, just who they were going to see. The rest is history. It's
been said Moe himself oversaw the auditioners, one by one, and personally
selected Marjorie for the role of Mary.

One can tell from the bubbly joie de vie in her composure and that
beautiful smile that can't be faked, that she was at her prime, enjoying
what she was doing, and simply having fun, probably more than ever
before in her life. She was poised for the big screen; she knew it, and
getting herself ready to tackle it. She was no longer the cutesy little girl
of the Winnipeg Kiddies, or one half of the White Sisters, but matur-
ing into a true beauty of the screen. She knew that, too, and made no
secret of how to use those qualities that she possessed and that the
public adored.

But such good fortune was not to be…

A couple of freeze-frames from Woman Haters,
just for her smile.

The Accident

On the evening of August 20, 1935, Marjorie, husband Ed, and friends Marlow Lovell, Gloria Gould, and William Mackie were enjoying a night on the town. En route from a party at Malibu Beach on the Roosevelt Highway (which today is Highway 101/I-405, the San Diego Freeway) near the Bel-Air Country Club (still there, today, as matter of fact) to another location, fate stepped in.

They were in two separate cars, one an open car, the other a closed model. Gloria was seated in the open car and at the last minute, because it was rather chilly, traded places with Marjorie in the closed car, because Gloria hadn't brought along her coat. As they traveled along, the open car, with Marlow and Marjorie inside, collided with another, that of Mr. and Mrs. Charles Marchesi. Lovell's car overturned. Marjorie was thrown out, and the car rolled over on top of her, crushing her beneath, and inflicting massive injuries. According to the transcript of the accident report and the later Coroner Inquest, Mr. Marchesi was absolved of any wrongdoing, but Marlow Lovell was cited as the cause of the accident due to careless driving. Marjorie was conscious when medics arrived, and able to tell them her name and address and other information, they rushed her to a Los Angeles hospital. Marjorie was bleeding internally and in a state of shock: doctors and surgeons worked feverishly through the night, but were unable to save her. She died at 7:25am on August 21, 1935, at age 31.[11]

The following excerpt is from Thelma's book, pages 158 and 159:

"One morning I had reported to Paramount for the first day's shooting on Never Too Late with Dick Talmadge. I was in the middle of a scene when I was called off the set to the telephone, something only allowed in exteme emergencies. My heart beating wildly, I picked up the receiver. 'Thelma? This is Eddie. Eddie Tierney.' 'Yes, Eddie.' 'Marjorie's been injured in a car wreck.' 'Oh, Eddie. How bad is she?' 'Pretty bad, the

doctor says. She's in St. Vincent's.' 'I'll be over as soon as I can.' 'I thought you'd want to know.' 'Yes, of course. Thanks, Eddie. I'll come as soon as I finish work tonight.'

"I replaced the receiver and sat a moment, stunned by the news. Even though Marjorie and I hadn't been close and I hadn't seen her for some time, I was still very upset. I finished at the studio and hurried home to change before going to the hospital. I was sitting at my dresser, putting the final touches to my makeup, and listening to the seven o'clock news on the radio. 'Finally, news from Hollywood,' came the impersonal voice at my elbow. 'A few hours ago, Marjorie White passed away from injuries received in an automobile accident early this morning. Miss White will be remembered for her many roles in motion pictures, notably Sunny Side Up…Movietone Follies of 1930…*and…' I dropped my lipstick on the dresser and leaned over to switch off the radio. Through my mind flashed the times we spent together, the hardships and the happiness, the fights and the fun we had, and I heard Mother's voice echo in my mind… "She needs all the love we can give her, baby."*

On that day the stage and screen lost a talented promising actress, and the world lost a warm, vibrant young woman who could have become one of the biggest stars of her day. Let's not forget her, but cherish her memory and celebrate the smiles she brought us. God keeps her soul.

Notes

1. Manitoba census records for the year 1911 show both Robert and wife Nettie, *nee* Roe, listing their places-of-birth as Ontario Province, disproving the error that he was a Scotland-born railroad worker to Canada. Her mother was of Irish descent, and the family adhered to the Presbyterian faith.

2. Can anyone guess the later stage name of Pincus Leff (1907-1993). He became Pinky Lee, the famous children's entertainer of the 1950s, distant forerunner of Pee-wee Herman, and who became famous in TV history for suffering the first heart attack on live television (though it was later reported to be a severe sinus attack).

3. Although he had been running his "Follies" shows at the Amsterdam since at least 1907, and in 1920-21 did two numbers with the name "Frolics," there is no reference of these two men in those numbers, although Will Rogers is credited as part of the "Ziegfeld Follies" of 1924 and 1925.

4. Photos such as this one were and still are common practice of movie studios for new hires. A series of study shots is taken, sans makeup, simply just-in-off-street "civilian" poses for studies of makeup, camera angles, etc. It is here that we see the *real* Marjorie, not the flapper or blonde movie star.

5. I find this film, on the whole, personally offensive to my taste for two glaringly obvious reasons: The first is the way her character is treated, especially the scene in the clubhouse when Tom Patricola discovers Marjorie is a girl not a boy, and physically throws her across the room to land in a heap in the corner. The other is the huge extravaganza production sequence with horrid blackface impersonations by all the white actors. This was done, presumably, to use Technicolor and the "Grandeur" (wide-screen) technique showing the actors' faces changing color from

shot to shot. I wonder: Was Marjorie part of that atrocious experiment? I certainly hope not. An article in the *Toronto Star*, March 1930, quotes her as saying she disliked the way she was treated so badly she would never do a cross-dressing part again.

6. I personally consider El Brendel as the singularly un-funniest comic of all time. To my taste, he makes Wheeler and Woolsey appear as Laurence Olivier and John Gielgud playing Shakespeare.

7. A son was born April 1930 to her brother Orville and his wife in Toronto. I find this very interesting for the following reason: with that child born in 1930, in his adult years he would have a family of his own, and his children would today be roughly aged 60 (the age of your author at this writing). If their offspring have children and grandchildren, as I do, this means I've opened the doors on six generations (to date 2008) of Marjorie White's family. I find this simply astounding, and emotionally rewarding.

8. This photo is among the rarest of my collection because it's one of only three candid shots I have of her, and the only full-face close-up.

9. This is another film I find so horrendously *bad* it's almost physically painful to watch. Aside from its shoddy storyline, try sitting through an hour or so of Bela Lugosi meowing like a cat, and El Brendel picking his nose, and see if you don't agree. How did poor Marjorie get stuck in a bowser like this one?

10. It has been said that Moe Howard supervised the auditions and personally selected Marjorie for the part.

11. Without going into grisly detail of her terrible injuries, people today incurring the same injuries, with today's medical science, are usually able to be healed and recover, but in 1935, sadly, this was not the case, and Marjorie succumbed.

Thelma's Book

Harry Preston is a veteran author and screenwriter, formerly with MGM Studios, with many books and films to his credit. He lives in Texas, and teaches screenwriting at Richland College. He received a Life Achievement Award at the Corpus Christi Film Festival for his contributions to the Texas film industry. He has written dozens of films and more than ninety books on films.

Much of the details of Marjorie's personal life I learned from reading Thelma White's biography *Thelma Who? Almost 100 Years of Showbiz*, written by author Harry Preston (seen here, at right). Through the kindness of the book's publisher Scarecrow Press, of Lanham, Maryland, I was able to contact Harry to tell him of what I was doing, and to ask him if he had any further information on Marjorie, not printed in the book. In the course of our pleasant conversation, this is what he told me:

He and Thelma's husband had been close buddies many years before, during their days together in Africa. In the early 1960s or thereabouts, they wound up living nearby each other in the L.A. area. They got together, and in the course of their meetings, she re-hashed all her old memories of the early days, her life and career and her relationship with Marjorie. He took down everything in notes, and they sat, untouched for about 40 years, when he dusted them off and put them into book form.

According to Harry's notes, she told him that in the mid-1950s, after having been sidelined by ill health for several years, she approached an

Thelma in 1997.

agent with the hope of getting back into show business. The puzzled agent asked her, "Thelma *WHO?*" Thus the book's title was born. Out of respect to Thelma's memory and so as not to plagiarize Harry's work, every excerpt from that book that I use in my own work here, is fully credited to both of them, in detail. (How I wish I had started this project a few years earlier while Thelma was still alive — she passed away in 2005 — that I'D be able to talk with her. Oh, but the things she could tell.)

Thelma in the 1930s.

Marjorie and Thelma.

Personal Family Photos

Get ready for a real treat: something very dear and special to me. My heartfelt thanks and appreciation go out to Ms. Marcine Jones of North Dakota, a distant cousin of Thelma Wolpa, who read my query about Marjorie in *Reminisce* magazine. Ms. Jones had these photos taken from her personal family album, restored, and sent to me by mail with her best wishes for my success in this work. The pictures here are Thelma and Marjorie as children — Ms. Jones is not sure of the dates. I spoke with her by phone right after receiving them to thank her. Believe me, when I opened the envelope and saw them, my heart skipped a beat, and I almost began to cry.

These pictures are but part of the larger group she sent, featuring more recent photos of Thelma in later years, with her mother Myrtle and one of her husbands and assorted friends, up into the 1960s, including Fifi D'Orsay, all at home together. Ms. Jones is the one and only living connection I have with Marjorie and Thelma.

Thelma is the taller, thinner of the two; Marjorie is the "punkin' cheeks" tot on the right. In my gratitude for her generosity in sharing these family heirlooms with me, I'll be sending her a copy of the finished work to enjoy the memories.

Ms. Jones was born several years after Marjorie's passing, and she told me that because of the distance between her and the Wolpa family, she had only met Thelma twice in her life. These photos are absolutely irreplaceable treasures. There exist numerous pictorials of celebrities, including childhood photos, but the pictures you see here have been quietly tucked away in a personal family album for generations. I'm very proud and pleased to know that I'm the first person to EVER see them, in almost 100 years. And with Ms. Jones' gracious permission, I'm pleased to be allowed to share them with the world.

Thank you ever so much Ms. Jones, and may God bless you.

Gary

Thelma and her mother Myrtle, about 1915 or 1916.

Marjorie and Thelma.

Thelma and Marjorie.

Thelma and Marjorie.

Thelma and Marjorie.

Main Street in downtown Winnipeg, 1905.

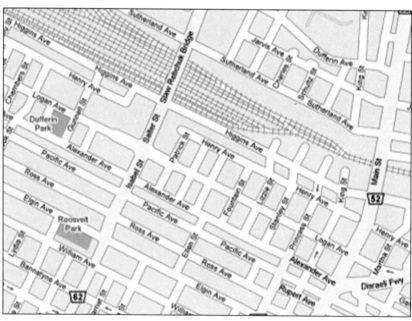

Winnipeg streets, 2005.

Winnipeg: Then and Now

All three streets lay within a mile or so of each other, and as can be seen by these over-views, both Pacific and William Avenues lie a bit to the west of Main Street, between Notre Dame Avenue to the south, and the rail yards to the north. This area was home to the Guthries in Marjorie's childhood.

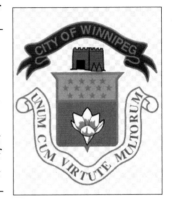

Studying the period pictures, and using my knowledge of urban development of most major cities, I've determined that Winnipeg was no different in its develop-ment from most others in North America in that period. With Main Street as the city's commercial hub, as we move outward even a short distance, the topography changes from the downtown edifices to semi-industrial areas, thinning out to residential neighborhoods, then small farm tracts to the edges of the city, then out to open agricultural country. I've gathered, by reading the classified ads of the period, under the listings for streets William and Pacific, that a great number of residences in that area were low-rent apartments and rooming houses, with a few small hotels spaced among them, providing lodging mostly for the workers and tradesmen of the area. I've been told by a knowledgeable historian of the Winnipeg Municipal Library that 151 Main Street, known as the Hespeler Block, was a small semi-residential complex of five or six units which held the facility of Dr. Jamieson (this verified by the Henderson's City Directory 1904-1911). It would appear then that, given the economic structure of the day, Marjorie's family was not wealthy by any means, but was actually merely scraping out a living from the father's labor, making barely enough to sustain a family of seven. They were poor folks, indeed, but in late years, she would surely make up for that poverty.

With the help of Google Search, I've been able to locate Marjorie's birthplace, and the area in which the family lived:

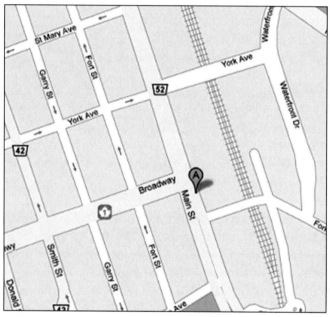

151 Main Street, at the corner of Broadway.

350 Pacific Avenue

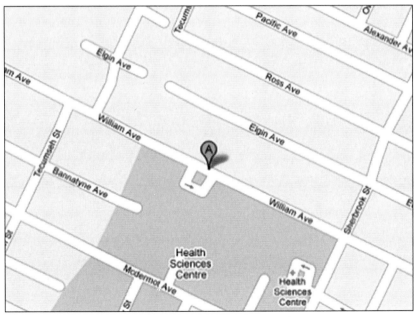

And later, 717 William Avenue

Winfield R. Sheehan
1883-1945

It was Sheehan (or one of his scouts) who spotted Marjorie in the play *Ladyfingers* at the Vanderbilt in early 1929, and immediately signed her to his Fox Studios to work in the musical *Sunny Side Up*, thus launching her film career. But biographical information on him is scarce, if not semi-nonexistant. The only photo I've been able to find came from an obscure book on American musical theater.

Born in Buffalo New York his first recorded film credit is as a supervisor of Howard Hawks' *Fig Leaves* for Fox in 1926. Sheehan was chief of production at the studio from the late 1920s to 1935, when the studio merged with Twentieth Century–a production firm established two years earlier by Joseph M. Schenck and Darryl F. Zanuck.

The text which follows was culled from www.*wikipedia.com:*

Winfield Sheehan (1883-1945) was a film company executive. He was responsible for much of Fox Film Corporation's output during the 1920s and 1930s. As studio head he won an Academy Award for Best Picture for the film *Cavalcade* and was nominated three more times. A native of Buffalo, New York, Sheehan served in the Spanish-American War as a teen. After working as a cub reporter he became a police reporter for New York's Evening World in the early 1900s. In 1910, Sheehan became the fire commissioner's secretary and in 1911 performed similar duties for the police commissioner. In the latter capacity, he helped the newly established studio of William Fox, stay afloat in the face of increasing pressure to fold from the Motion Picture Patents Company, which routinely absorbed, intimidated, and ultimately destroyed most fledgling studios. The Fox case played a vital role in the destruction of the Motion Picture Patents Company's absolute control.

Afterward, Sheehan became William Fox's personal secretary and two years later became the studio's general manager and vice president. He then served as Fox's chief of production until 1935 when the studio became part of 20th Century-Fox and was replaced by Darryl Zanuck. After that, Sheehan became an independent producer until his death in 1945.

Also (source unknown):

Studio executive Winfield Sheehan was closely associated with 20th Century Fox Studios. A native of Buffalo, New York, Sheehan served in the Spanish-American War in his teens. After working as a cub reporter he became a police reporter for *New York's Evening World* in the early 1900s. In 1910, he became the fire commissioner's secretary and in 1911 performed similar duties for the police commissioner.

In the latter capacity, he helped the newly established studio of William Fox stay afloat in the face of increasing pressure to fold from the Motion Picture Patents Company, which routinely absorbed, intimidated, and ultimately destroyed most fledgling studios. The Fox case played a vital role in the destruction of the Motion Picture Patents Company's absolute control. Afterward, Sheehan became William Fox's personal secretary and two years later became the studio's general manager and vice president. He then served as Fox's chief of production until 1935 when the studio became part of 20th Century. After that, Sheehan became an independent producer. After his departure from Fox in 1935, he continued in the business industry until his death in 1945.

I have tried, unsuccessfully, to search the records of 20th Century Fox, The Margaret Herrick Library of UCLA, and other sources to see if I could find anything on him, but with no luck at all. Even the New York City Public Library's Billy Rose Collection has but a small folio of his Fox business papers, nothing more. Feel free to contact me if you know of any source where I might find any of his company paperwork (contracts, etc.) relating to Marjorie White. Thanks.

In Closing...

I hope I've given everyone a bit of a glimpse into this woman's life of so long ago. Though long ago, the story of Marjorie White truly embodies the joys and sorrows, hopes and dreams of our lives today.

Even though she died thirteen years before I was born, in the course of this work I like to think I've come to know her as a living person, rather than an image seen only on a few minutes of grainy black-and-white film from years gone past. Before *Woman Haters,* I'd never seen or heard of her, but what struck me about her was her seemingly inborn *elan* and *joie de vie* that broke through the many dismal roles she played on film, shining like a bright star in the darkness. I think we'll agree (at least I hope so) that she was not necessarily a great actress, but amongst the most energetic and talented entertainers of her age. And for that reason alone, I decided to embark on the task of documenting her life so every comedy fan will come to know her as I have. I've spent the last few years on a virtual "time travel" trip through history, following this woman through the years of her life, "peekin' through the keyhole," as it were, and "waitin' in the wings," taking notes of her work. Over the years, I've learned to admire and respect the talents, crafts and skills that went into acting and film making of those long-ago days, the silents of the teens and twenties, and the early talkies of the thirties. I've become a dedicated observer of that era, adding so much to my pleasure watching those classic old films. So many talented people have come and gone over the past 100 years of film, so few are remembered today. For every John Wayne and Clark Gable there were dozens, if not hundreds of Dwight Fryes, Frank Albertsons, and Charles Farrells. For every Joan Crawford and Greta Garbo there were just as many Leila Hyams', Sally Eilers', and Marjorie Whites. That's why, in my opinion, Marjorie stands out as one who highly deserves to be remembered for her brief life and career on the stage and film. There are a number of areas I've opted to omit in my research on her (these I've discussed with author Harry Preston as well as a number of other fans), for several reasons: Even though she's been gone more than 75 years, I feel that to disclose anything more intimate about her personal life would be disrespectful to her memory and tarnish the shine she left behind. Even someone known only to history deserves her own bit of privacy. I hope you've enjoyed reading this piece as much as I have putting it together. If you have any questions regarding anything I've covered in these pages. Please contact me with anything you have on her that I don't. Anyone's contribution(s) to this work are much appreciated, I most certainly welcome them. Thanks again for your interest. *"MY LIFE, MY LOVE, MY ALL."*

Only the Beginning.

There's not much more I can come up with that hasn't been previously published, the remaining items are all the form of government documents of both the U.S. and Canada such as birth certificates, church and school records and other such paraphernalia to be used in print as footnotes, but mostly for my personal files, to verify dates and places. The Canadian Government has records dating to the 17th century, such as immigrations, tax records, land grants, etc., birth and census records to the 1860s, province by province, each with its own archival system, and although the people of those agencies are most cordially helpful, these records can, and do, take a lot of work to locate, and this takes time. If and when I acquire those documents, I'll issue an addendum to this book with all the pertinent information included.

Meanwhile, enjoy reading this one. I hope I've done the woman's life long-overdue justice.

Gary Olszewski
Las Vegas, Nevada
garysheski@ymail.com

About The Author

Gary Olszewski, an avid theater historian, began this book after seeing her play the lead in 1934's *Woman Haters,* billed top and above The Three Stooges, and started with the thought "Who was she, and whatever became of her?" Upon researching her life and career, he embarked on a comprehensive biographical/historical journey of her and her family ancestry, which dates to Scotland"s House of Stuart in the 1600s. Gary is a semi-retired Vietnam veteran, and currently lives in Las Vegas, Nevada, where he continues his literary pursuits.

Index

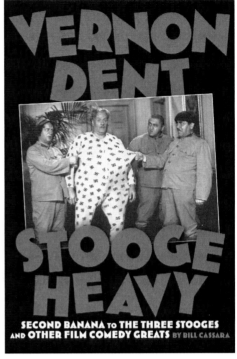

Made in United States
North Haven, CT
23 November 2021

11437856R00065